Facts About the Rat

By Lisa Strattin

© 2019 Lisa Strattin

FREE BOOK

FREE FOR ALL SUBSCRIBERS

LisaStrattin.com/Subscribe-Here

BOX SET

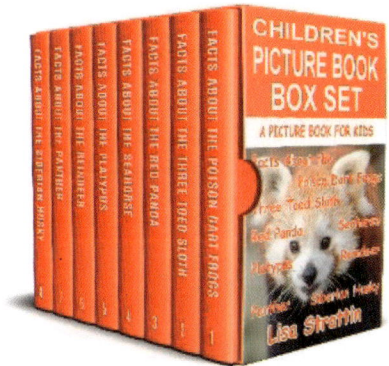

- **FACTS ABOUT THE POISON DART FROGS**
- **FACTS ABOUT THE THREE TOED SLOTH**
- **FACTS ABOUT THE RED PANDA**
- **FACTS ABOUT THE SEAHORSE**
- **FACTS ABOUT THE PLATYPUS**
- **FACTS ABOUT THE REINDEER**
- **FACTS ABOUT THE PANTHER**
- **FACTS ABOUT THE SIBERIAN HUSKY**

LisaStrattin.com/BookBundle

Facts for Kids Picture Books by Lisa Strattin

Little Blue Penguin, Vol 92

Chipmunk, Vol 5

Frilled Lizard, Vol 39

Blue and Gold Macaw, Vol 13

Poison Dart Frogs, Vol 50

Blue Tarantula, Vol 115

African Elephants, Vol 8

Amur Leopard, Vol 89

Sabre Tooth Tiger, Vol 167

Baboon, Vol 174

Sign Up for New Release Emails Here

LisaStrattin.com/subscribe-here

All rights reserved. No part of this book may be reproduced by any means whatsoever without the written permission from the author, except brief portions quoted for purpose of review.

All information in this book has been carefully researched and checked for factual accuracy. However, the author and publisher makes no warranty, express or implied, that the information contained herein is appropriate for every individual, situation or purpose and assume no responsibility for errors or omissions. The reader assumes the risk and full responsibility for all actions, and the author will not be held responsible for any loss or damage, whether consequential, incidental, special or otherwise, that may result from the information presented in this book.

All images are free for use or purchased from stock photo sites or royalty free for commercial use.

Some coloring pages might be of the general species due to lack of available images.

I have relied on my own observations as well as many different sources for this book and I have done my best to check facts and give credit where it is due. In the event that any material is used without proper permission, please contact me so that the oversight can be corrected.

COVER IMAGE

By Michael Palmer - Own work, CC BY-SA 4.0, https://commons.wikimedia.org/w/index.php?curid=37119619

ADDITIONAL IMAGES

https://www.flickr.com/photos/liftarn/8881828395/

https://www.flickr.com/photos/43158397@N02/4491436430/

https://www.flickr.com/photos/genista/2388754/

https://www.flickr.com/photos/liftarn/15505768328/

https://www.flickr.com/photos/amylloyd/32894111532/

https://www.flickr.com/photos/155733895@N04/38657027291/

Contents

INTRODUCTION 9

CHARACTERISTICS 11

APPEARANCE 13

REPRODUCTION 15

LIFE SPAN 17

SIZE 19

HABITAT 21

DIET 23

ENEMIES 25

SUITABILITY AS PETS 27

INTRODUCTION

The two most common species of rat are the black rat and the brown rat and they are found all over the world. The rat is generally found in small, dark places and is thought to have originated in Asia before migrating across countries and being accidental passengers on human voyages on ships. The rat is now one of the most widely spread and adaptable animals in the world.

CHARACTERISTICS

The rat is a small scavenger mammal that has proved to be a pest. They are known to kill smaller livestock on farms.

The rat can also carry and spread disease to a devastating effect. As a matter of fact, in the Middle Ages, the Black Plague wiped out nearly two thirds of the people in European countries. The disease was not caused by the rats directly but was actually caused by the infected fleas carried on rats.

APPEARANCE

Rats are generally slender, with a pointed head, large eyes, and prominent, lightly furred ears. They have moderately long legs and long, sharp claws. The soles of their feet have no fur.

REPRODUCTION

Rats are fast breeders and give birth to large litters of babies, usually 6 to 10 at a time. This means that pet rats of different genders should be separated at around a month old. They are able to start having babies at around 5 weeks of age after a gestation period of only 22 days .Although rats can live until they are 4 or 5 years old, females can no longer have babies after they are about 18 months old.

LIFE SPAN

Rats live for 2 to 5 years.

SIZE

The most distinctive difference between rats and mice is their size. Rats tend to be much larger than mice. They can be between 8 to 19 inches long as adults and weigh up to 2 pounds.

HABITAT

Rats thrive almost anywhere where food and shelter are available for them. They are found nesting in and around homes, warehouses, office buildings, barns, cellars, sewers, garbage dumps, and other areas that provide ample food. They are opportunistic eaters, which means they will eat pretty much any food or garbage left out by people that they find.

DIET

Rats are omnivorous animals and eat a mixture of plant and meat in order to get all the right nutrients to thrive. They are known to eat almost anything and with the high trash levels in cities, there has been a new generation of oversized super rats in some cities. The large rats are much bigger than the average rat and are more dominant in their environment.

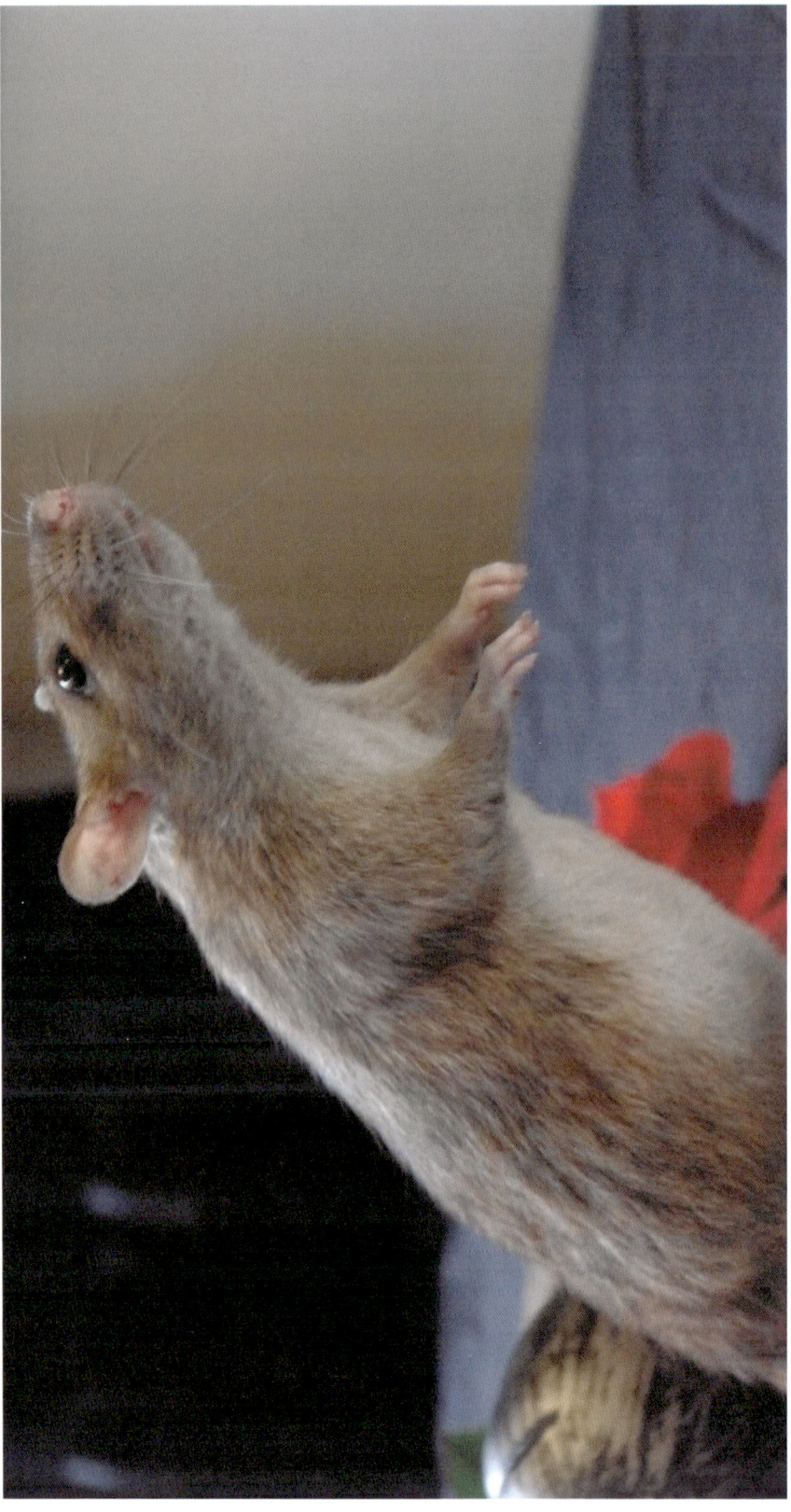

ENEMIES

In the wild, rats are preyed upon by many different animals including snakes, wildcats and birds of prey.

SUITABILITY AS PETS

Today, rats are commonly kept as pets all over the world and are thought to have been bred as pets since the 1800s.

Pet rats pose the same health risks to humans as other household animals so are not considered to carry harmful diseases. When tame, rats can be extremely friendly and can be taught to perform selective tasks such as doing certain actions in order to get food.

If you choose to have a rat as a pet, you might be pleasantly surprised at how much fun they can be!

COLOR ME

COLOR ME

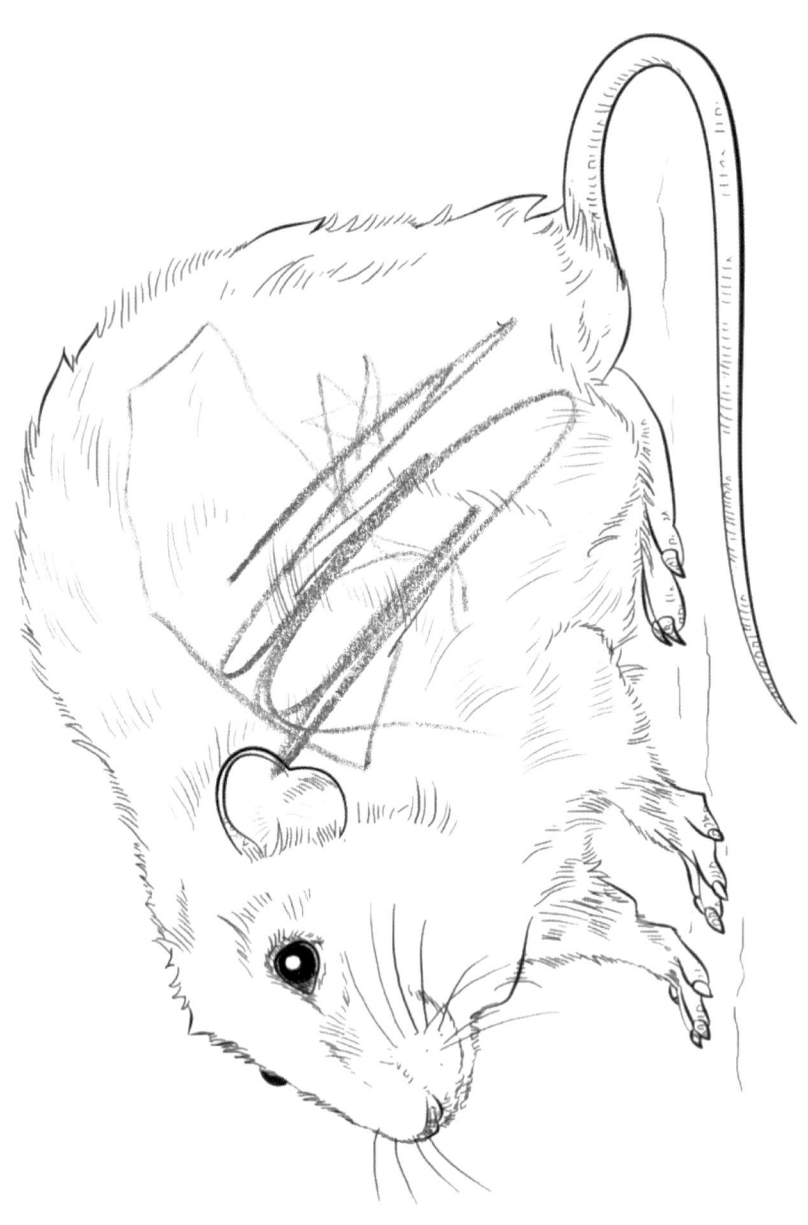

30

COLOR ME

COLOR ME

32

COLOR ME

COLOR ME

COLOR ME

COLOR ME

COLOR ME

37

COLOR ME

Please leave me a review here:

LisaStrattin.com/Review-Vol-258

For more Kindle Downloads Visit Lisa Strattin Author Page on Amazon Author Central

amazon.com/author/lisastrattin

To see upcoming titles, visit my website at LisaStrattin.com– most books available on Kindle!

LisaStrattin.com

FREE BOOK

FOR ALL SUBSCRIBERS – SIGN UP NOW

LisaStrattin.com/Subscribe-Here

LisaStrattin.com/Facebook

LisaStrattin.com/Youtube

Printed in Great Britain
by Amazon